The Surname Moffat

Susan Morris &
Wendy Bosberry-Scott

ISBN: 1540499367
ISBN-13: 978-1540499363

The question of surnames, their origins, distribution and history, lies at the heart of genealogy as well as being fascinating in its own right.

In the 1980s and 1990s, long before many genealogical sources were even indexed, let alone online, our Surname Report service provided expert assessments of the origins, history and distribution of selected British surnames, using the sources available at the time.

Now, with so many more sources available, we believe that these reports retain their value as studies of individual surnames, and so we are gradually making the Debrett Surname Archive available online and in print for the first time. Some modern indexes have been consulted to refresh and update the reports.

Debrett Ancestry Research Ltd, PO Box 379,
Winchester SO23 9YQ
Tel: 01962 841904
Email: info@debrettancestry.co.uk
Website: www.debrettancestry.co.uk

CONTENTS

1   Overview   1

2   Origins and Early Examples   3

3   Distribution   6

4   Famous Bearers of the Name   15

5   Printed Genealogies   17

6   Summary   18

7   Sources Consulted   19

Overview

The use of surnames in England began in the Norman period, when surnames were not necessarily hereditary but usually a form of description. Some described the individual's trade or profession; others were nicknames; some gave the father's Christian name; others gave the individual's place of residence or origin.

Different surnames might be used in different documents, or more than one surname given in one document. Early descriptions were fairly elaborate and by the thirteenth and fourteenth centuries these were simpler, but still variable, and indeed the instability of surnames continued until well into the seventeenth century.

Although some Normans would already have had hereditary surnames on their arrival in Britain, the passing on of a surname from generation to generation only became customary in Britain gradually during the course of the thirteenth and fourteenth centuries. At the end of this period most of the population apparently had surnames.

Variations in the spelling of a family's surname continue to be found until the present century. Before this, as most people could not read or write, the parish clerk or other official would write down the name as they heard it.

There are four main groups of surnames:

A – Local names, which describe a person by his place of residence or origin.

B – Occupational names, which describe a person by his trade or profession.

C – Surnames of relationship, which refer to the Christian name of the father or other important relative.

D – Nicknames or sobriquets, coined to describe a person in terms of his appearance or character.

Many surnames have uncertain origins, but the name Moffat clearly falls into Category A.

Origins and early examples

Our research into the surname Moffat has found it to be common in southern Scotland. In Scotland, the surname Moffatt derives from the place-name Moffat in Annandale, Dumfriesshire. Patrick Hanks and Flavia Hodges, in their *Dictionary of Surnames* (1988), give the origin of the place-name Moffat as the gaelic *magh* meaning 'plain' or 'field' and *fada* meaning 'long'.

The earliest example of the name Moffat comes from before 1232 when one Nicholas de Mufet, a cleric, witnessed a charter drawn up by Walter, bishop of Glasgow (*Liber Cartarum Sancte Crucus*, Edinburgh 1840, pg 55). In 1250 the same Nicholas de Mufet was recorded as archdeacon of Theuidale (*Liber S. Marie de Calchou; registrum cartarum abbacie Tironesnsis de Kelso*, Edinburgh 1846, 2 volumes, pgs 148, 149) and in 1268 he was elected bishop of Glasgow, but he died in 1270 before consecration (*The Bishops of Scotland*, John Dowden DD, Glasgow 1912, pg 305).

Other early examples of the surname appearing in early Scottish records are as follows:

| 1296 | Robert de Muffet | rendered homage (of Dumfriesshire) and inquisitor re lands (1303) |
| 1296 | Thomas Moffet | rendered homage (of Dumfriesshire) |

| 1348 | Walter de Moffat | Miscellany of the Spalding Club |
| 1467 | Robert de Moffethe | *Registrum Episcopatus Glasguensis* |

Walter de Moffat was the archdeacon of Lothian in 1348 and Robert de Moffethe was the treasurer of the church of Glasgow in 1467. Black notes that 'the Moffettis of the West Marche' were recorded as one of the 'unruly Border clans' in 1587 (*The Acts of Parliament of Scotland 1124-1701*).

Black noted the following variants of the name Moffat: Maffit and Moffit 1868, Moffot 1520, Muffett 1583 and Mwffett 1593.

P H Reaney (*Dictionary of English Surnames*, 1995) cites the two earliest examples provided by Black (see above) and groups Moffat with the variants Moffet, Moffitt, Muffatt, Muffett, Meffatt and Meffet.

M A Lower's *Patronymica Brittanica* (1860), an early but still valuable British surname dictionary, only shows the name as Moffatt and states that it derives from 'a parish partly in Dumfriesshire and partly in Lanarkshire'.

C W Bardsley, in his *Dictionary of English and Welsh Surnames* (1901), agrees that the origins of the surname Moffat(t) lie in the Dumfriesshire parish. In his survey of directories he found that the name Moffat was listed in an 1870 edition of a London directory twice and Moffatt was listed ten times, whereas an 1877 edition of a New York directory found eleven entries for Moffat and seven for Moffatt.

4

During the course of our research we have found the variants Moffot(t), Muffit, Muffitt, Mofatta and Maffot. We found a single reference to the form Moffoot. However, it is likely that Moffoot is rather a variant of the English topographical surname Moorfoot. P H Reaney (1995) found a Robert Morfot in Lincolnshire Assize Rolls in 1373-5 and a George Morfotte in Sussex Subsidy Rolls in 1525, for which he suggests the derivation 'dweller at the foot of the moor' (Old English *mor fot*).

Distribution

Moffat is a Scottish name, but one that has spread widely. Richard McKinley cites it in his *History of British Surnames* (1990) as an example of a locative surname that has ramified in southern Scotland. He suggests that surnames that did this often belonged to the moderately prosperous members of society such as yeomen or 'minor gentry', who were likely to have large numbers of healthy children. McKinley also notes that most of such families had already divided into a number of branches by around 1400.

In 1890 H B Guppy published his *Homes of Family Names in Great Britain*, still the only printed work on surname distribution in Britain as a whole. His work was based on printed genealogies and a survey of county directories for the 1880s, in which he looked especially at the names of farmers, reasoning that they were among the most stable groups in society.

Guppy restricted his study to names which appeared in a proportion of 7:10,000 or higher. Guppy observed that the name Moffat or Moffatt was best represented on the Scottish side of the England/Scotland border. He noted that there was a proportion of 39:10,000 farmers who used the name Moffatt at that time in Cumberland and Westmoreland, and 11:10,000 in Northumberland. In Scotland, he found that 17:10,000 farmers used the name Moffat in the south of Forth and the Clyde, especially on the Scottish border in Dumfrieshire.

In a *Special Report on Surnames of Ireland* (1909) the Registrar-General Sir Robert E Matheson, published a survey of the births registered in Ireland in 1890 which lists the numbers of births registered for all names which appear in the indexes more than five times. Moffat (*etc*) appeared 68 times. There were seven births registered in the Leinster district, 45 in Ulster and 16 in Connaught. The breakdown of numbers for the variants is as follows:

Moffatt	17
Moffat	11
Moffett	12
Moffet	10
Moffitt	11
Moffit	7

Sir Robert found that the name Moffat was principally found in the Counties Antrim, Sligo and Tyrone. Edward MacLysaght, in his more general work *Surnames of Ireland* (1977), described Moffat as a Scottish name that has been numerous in Ulster since the early seventeenth century.

Many of the sources available for charting surname distribution through the centuries are necessarily confined to the wealthier sectors of the population: in general, nobody wanted to know the names of the poor but the names of those with money or land were naturally of interest to the authorities. However, one source that covers the whole of the social spectrum is provided by English parish registers, the earliest of which began in 1538 following a mandate that all parish priests should keep a weekly record of all baptisms, marriages and burials that took place in their parish. A

7

survey of a cross section of parish registers for the years 1601 and 1602 was carried out in 1910 by F K and S Hitching; incidences of a particular surname are noted by parish and county, although with no indication of numbers of references.

There were no relevant entries found in the 1601 index but the name Moffet was found in the baptismal registers of Whickham in County Durham in 1602.

A useful guide to the distribution of surnames for the sixteenth, seventeenth and eighteenth centuries in England is provided by the indexes to wills proved, and administrations granted, at the Prerogative Court of (the Archbishop of) Canterbury, in London, which had superior jurisdiction over local ecclesiastical courts where wills were proved until 1858. The PCC thus provides a national index, although it is not a completely representative one, as testators whose wills were proved in the PCC were mostly among the wealthier members of society, and a disproportionate number of them were from London or Middlesex.

A search of the indexes for the years 1584 to 1800 found numerous entries for Moffat(t) with some examples of Muffett, Moffett, Moffitt and Moffata:

1558-1599
1597   John Muffett, of St Leonard, Shoreditch, Middlesex

Seventeenth Century
1604   Thomas Moffet, Wilton, Wiltshire
1624   Gasper Moffata, beyond the seas
1661   Mary Moffett, widow of Endfield, Middlesex

1674 John Moffett, Neata Mariae Savoy, Middlesex
1677 John Moffitt, mariner of Wapping, Middlesex
1680 David Muffett, mariner of Levin, Fife (died on
      ship Formioza, *Pts*)
1685 Thomas Moffett, citizen & grocer of St
      Stephen, Coleman Street, London
1696 William Muffet or Muffitt, mariner TMS
      London (died on ship Breda)

Eighteenth Century
1759 Walter Moffett, Middlesex
1761 John Moffett, *Pts*
1763 James Moffott, Middlesex
1763 William Moffatt, of Devon, died *Pts*
1764 Mary Moffatt, Huntingdonshire
1764 Walter Moffett, *Pts*
1769 James Moffett, *Pts*
1769 George Muffet, Middlesex
1775 Robert Muffett, London
1776 Elizabeth Muffett, Middlesex
1777 James Moffatt, Middlesex
1779 Thomas Moffett, *Pts*
1780 Radcliffe Moffatt, Middlesex
1780 Andrew Moffatt Esq, Essex
1782 William Maffot, *Pts*
1782 Willaim Moffatt, *Pts*
1783 John Moffatt, Service, *Pts*
1783 James Moffett, London
1783 Henry Moffitt, *Pts*
1785 Robert Muffett, London
1786 Thomas Moffatt, Devon
1787 Thomas Moffat, Doctor of Physics, Middlesex
1790 James Moffatt Esq, Kent
1790 James Moffat, Middlesex
1791 Robert Moffett, Middlesex
1793 John Moffat, *Pts*
1798 Jane Moffat, Jersey
1798 James Thomas Moffett, London

1798   Aaron Moffatt Esq, *Pts*
1799   Adam Moffatt, ship Gorgon, *Pts*
1799   Elizabeth Moffatt, Middlesex
1799   Elizabeth Moffat, Southampton

1800-1857
1800   James Moffat, North Britain [Scotland]
1800   John Moffat, Middlesex
1800   John Moffatt, London

The PCC was the usual court used for testators who died abroad and there are fifteen such examples here; these people died *in partibus (transmarinis)*, signified by *'Pts'*. One, William Moffatt whose will was proved in 1763, came from Devon; the only other will proved for a testator from Devon was in 1786, for Thomas Moffatt. There are two examples of the name as Moffot(t) here: James Moffott of Middlesex, whose will was proved in 1763 and William Moffot who died in foreign parts and whose will was proved in 1782.

From this list, the concentration of the name appears to be in the south-eastern area of England, with the highest concentration of the name in Middlesex and London, but this in part reflects the fact that the court was situated in London; by the eighteenth century the PCC was increasingly used by families of all walks of life in the metropolitan area.

For the nineteenth century, H B Guppy's survey has been mentioned above. Another important Victorian source is the *Return of Owners of Land of 1873*, sometimes known as the Modern Domesday Book. This source lists, county by county, every owner of an acre of land or more, with their residence and the acreage of their holding:

Return of Owners of Land

Cumberland	4	Moffat
	2	Moffatt
	1	Moffitt
Herefordshire	1	Moffatt
Kent	1	Muffett
Lincolnshire	2	Moffatt
Northumberland	1	Moffat
	1	Moffatt
Oxfordshire	1	Moffatt
Suffolk	1	Moffatt
Warwickshire	1	Moffatt
Westmoreland	3	Moffat
Yorkshire North	1	Moffitt
Yorkshire West	1	Moffatt
	1	Muffitt

No examples of Moffo(o)t(t) were found during this search. Moffat(t) was found in the northern areas of the country and reached only as far south as Herefordshire, Warwickshire and Suffolk. The only variant found in the south was in Kent and then only one person was found with the name Muffett. The highest concentration of the name in this list was found in Cumberland, the county bordering Dumfriesshire.

The first decennial census return in England, Scotland and Wales was taken in 1801, but personal information was only recorded from 1841 onwards. From 1851, the age, occupation and birthplace is given for each member of the household, and so these records provide

11

invaluable genealogical information as well as a fascinating 'snapshot' of the family in the nineteenth century. The latest return currently open to public inspection is that of 1911 and there are now national indexes to the returns from 1841 onwards, although these indexes are not wholly reliable. Using these indexes, we found the following numbers for Moffat(t), Moffitt, Moffo(o)tt and Muffitt in England and Scotland:

ENGLAND

6 June 1841
Moffat (535); Moffatt (579); Moffitt (201); Moffoot (10); Moffott (9): Muffitt (62)

30 March 1851
Moffat (793); Moffatt (813); Moffitt (255); Moffoot (14); Moffott (15); Muffitt (50)

7 April 1861
Moffat (911); Moffatt (1000); Moffitt (244); Moffoot (15); Moffott (15); Muffitt (78)

2 April 1871
Moffat (1120); Moffatt (1247); Moffitt (394); Moffoot (20); Moffott (1); Muffitt (47)

3 April 1881
Moffat (1411); Moffatt (1725); Moffitt (490); Moffoot (15); Moffott (8); Muffitt (81)

5 April 1891
Moffat (1669); Moffatt (1967); Moffitt (487); Moffoot (20); Moffott (11); Muffitt (24)

31 March 1901
Moffat (1662); Moffatt (2418); Moffitt (596); Moffoot (13); Moffott (5); Muffitt (42)

2 April 1911
Moffat (2033); Moffatt (2257); Moffitt (739); Moffoot (25); Moffott (4); Muffitt (133)

SCOTLAND

6 June 1841
Moffat (2755); Moffatt (60)

30 March 1851
Moffat (3232); Moffatt (78); Moffo(o)t(t) (0)

7 April 1861
Moffat (3211); Moffatt (147)

2 April 1871
Moffat (3606); Moffatt (186); Moffott (3); Moffoot (0)

3 April 1881
Moffat (4062); Moffatt (216)

5 April 1891
Moffat (4439); Moffatt (210); Moffo(o)t(t) (0)

31 March 1901
Moffat (4876); Moffatt (331)

2 April 1911
Moffat (5087); Moffatt (335); Moffitt (9);
Moffo(o)t/Muffitt (0)

Moffat was by far the form most widely found in Scotland, but in England Moffatt was more common. The general increase between 1841 and 1911 reflects of course the rapidly expanding population in this period. Numbers for Moffott and Moffoot were so low that a single family might account for all the instances in each case. These forms were scarcely found in Scotland.

Famous bearers of the name

In *Debrett's People of Today (1996)* the following references were found for Moffat and Moffatt:

> Alexander Moffat, artist and photographer
> Alistair Murray Moffat, organiser of the Edinburgh Fringe Festival
> Lt-Gen Sir William Cameron Moffat KBE, retired military surgeon
> David A Moffat, surgeon
> Gwen Mary Moffat, author
> Dr Robin John Russell Moffat, police surgeon & forensic examiner
> Sheilagh Moffat, chartered accountant
> Clive Moffatt, economist
> Professor Henry Keith Moffatt, mathematician
> Nigel Moffatt, playwright & poet
> Dr William Henry Moffatt OBE, retired consultant physician in geriatrics
> Steven Moffat, playwright and producer

The *Dictionary of National Biography* for the British Isles lists the following Moffat *etc* entries:

> Robert Moffat, missionary (Dr Livingstone's father in law) (1795-1833)
> John Marks Moffatt, antiquarian (d1802)
> Thomas Moffett, physician and author (1553-1604)
> James Moffatt, theologian (1870-1944)

There is one coat of arms listed in Burke's *General Armory* (1884) granted to a man of the name Moffat, two to men of the name Moffatt and one of the name Moffett.

Moffat (that Ilk, Annandale) Sable a saltire and chief argent (sometimes argent a saltire azure and chief gules).

Moffatt (Goodrich Court, Herefordshire) Argent a saltire gules and a chief azure.
Crest - The sun in splendour proper

Moffatt (Lauder, Herefordshire) Argent a lion rampant sable between eight escallops in orle gules

Moffett (Chipping Barnet, Hertfordshire; granted 10 May 1585) Same *Arms* a rose or for difference.

Printed Genealogies

The following references to Moffat, Moffatt, Moffett, Moffitt and Maffett have been noted:

Maffett
E Hamilton, *Hamilton Memoirs*, (1920) 51

Moffat(t)
R M Moffatt, *A Short History of the Family of Moffatt of that Ilk*, (1908)
Burke's Colonial Gentry, i, 184
Burkes' Landed Gentry, 7, 8
Burke's Distinguished Families of the USA

Moffett, Moffitt
R M Moffatt, *A Short History of the Family of Moffatt of that Ilk*, (1908) 86, 93, 97a

Summary

To conclude, the surname Moffat is of Scottish origin and derives from the place-name Moffat in Dumfriesshire.

Sources Consulted

P H Reaney, *The Origins of English Surnames* (London: Routledge & Kegan Paul, 1967)

P H Reaney & R M Wilson, *A Dictionary of British Surnames* (Oxford: Oxford University Press, 3rd edition, 1995)

P H Reaney, *Dictionary of British Surnames* (London: Routledge & Kegan Paul, 2nd edition, 1976)

P Hanks & F Hodges, *A Dictionary of Surnames* (Oxford University Press, 1988)

M A Lower, *Patronymica Brittanica* (London, 1860)

C W Bardsley, *Dictionary of English and Welsh Surnames* (1901: reprinted, Baltimore: Genealogical Publishing Co, 1967)

C L'Estrange Ewen, *Guide to the Origin of British Surnames* (London: John Gifford, 1938)

H B Guppy, *Homes of Family Names in Great Britain* (London, 1890)

Ernest Weekley, *The Romance of Names* (London: John Murray, 2nd edition, 1917)

Ernest Weekley, *Surnames* (London: John Murray, 1917)

George F Black, *The Surnames of Scotland* (New York Public Library, 1946)

Edward McLysaght, *The Surnames of Ireland* (Dublin: Irish University Press, 1977)

T J & Prys Morgan, *Welsh Surnames* (Cardiff: University of Wales Press, 1985)

F K & S Hitching, *References to English Surnames in 1601* (Walton on Thames: Bernau, 1910)

F K & S Hitching, *References to English Surnames in 1602* (Walton on Thames: Bernau, 1911)

Debrett's People of Today (Debrett's Peerage Limited: London, 1996)

The Dictionary of National Biography: Index & Epitome (London, 1906)

The Concise Dictionary of National Biography, Part II, 1901–1950, (Oxford, 1961)

Burke's Family Index (London: Burke's Peerage Limited, 1976)

H R Moulton, *Palaeography, Genealogy & Topography* (Sale Catalogue, 1930)

Index to Prerogative Court of Canterbury Wills (The National Archives: online)

G W Marshall, *The Genealogist's Guide* (1903; reprinted, Baltimore: GPC 1973)

J B Whitmore, *A Genealogical Guide* (London, 1953)

Charles Bridge, *An Index to Pedigrees* (London, 1867)

Geoffrey B Barrow, *The Genealogist's Guide* (London: Research Publishing Co, 1977)

Sir Bernard Burke, *The General Armory* (London, 1884)

C R Humphrey-Smith, editor, *Burke's General Armory Volume II,* (Tabard Press, 1973)

The Return of Owners of Land (1873)

Eilert Ekwall, *The Concise Oxford Dictionary of English Place-Names* (Oxford: Clarendon Press, 4th edition, 1960)

E G Withycombe, *The Oxford Dictionary of English Christian Names* (Oxford: Clarendon Press, 2nd edition, 1950)

W J Hardy & W Page, *A Calendar to the Feet of Fines for London and Middlesex: Vol 1 Richard I – Richard III (1189–1485)* (London, 1892)

Richard McKinley, *The Surnames of Oxfordshire* (English Surnames Series III: Leopard's Head Press, 1977)

Richard McKinley, *The Surnames of Sussex* (English Surnames Series V: Leopard's Head Press, 1988)

Richard McKinley, *The Surnames of Lancashire* (English Surnames Series IV: Leopard's Head Press, 1981)

Richard McKinley, *Norfolk and Suffolk Surnames in the Middle Ages* (English Surnames Series II: Phillimore, 1975)

George Redmonds, *Yorkshire West Riding* (English Surnames Series I: Phillimore, 1973)

Mr Avenell, *The Norman People* (London, 1874)

Debrett's Heraldry (London, 1933)

J P Brooke-Little, revised, *Boutell's Heraldry* (Frederick Warne: London, 1970)

Indexes to 1841–1911 Census Returns of England and Wales (The National Archives/*Ancestry.com*)

Indexes to 1841–1911 Census Returns of Scotland (*ScotlandsPeople*)

www.ingramcontent.com/pod-product-compliance
Lightning Source LLC
Chambersburg PA
CBHW070251290526
45789CB00004B/1826